CW01238968

NAUGHTY KINKY & STUPID PICK-UP LINES YOU WON'T BELIEVE

DAMN YOU tinder

Damn You Tinder!
[Black & White]
Naughty, Kinky & Stupid Pick-up Lines You Won't Believe!
by Gordon Sutherland

Copyright © 2015 by Damn You Publishing Ltd.

Tinder , you most likely have heard about it. You may be already using the app. It is the ultimate form of dating these days and you won't believe how some people abuse the privilege. But no worries, that's exactly why this book exists - to show you the gloriously hilarious things that can happen when a modern dating app meets modern (yet confounded) humans.

You like taking just a little bit of pleasure in the misfortune of others? "Damn You, Tinder" guaranteed to put you on the floor laughing! It will leave you laughing until you cry, and thankful that nothing this embarrassing has happened to you. Yet.

Parents take caution - this book contains humor and words that are NOT suitable for children.

ISBN-13: 978-1-517-02056-9
ISBN-10: 1517020565

Book Website
www.damnyoupublishing.com

Give feedback & sent your fails to:
Email: info@damnyoupublishing.com

●●●○○ T-NAUGHTY 📶　　4:21 PM　　✳ 96% 🔋

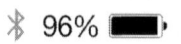

SMASHED PUSSY
NAUGHTY TINDER CHATS

Do you have pet insurance?

Haha no, but I have considerd it. Nice icebreaker. Do you?

No, I had a turtle but I got him a new tank and he died of some sort of infection 3 weeks later. :(

By the way, it's too bad you don't have pet insurance because your pussy is getting smashed tonight :)

Send

●●●○○ T-NAUGHTY 📶　　3:51 PM　　* 22% 🔋

DADDY IN JAIL
NAUGHTY TINDER CHATS

> Is your dad in Jail? Cus if I was your dad I'd be in jail

> That's not the creepiest thing I've heard, but it's still pretty sick. Not gonna work buddy

> So..dtf?

DTF = "down to fuck"

Send

•••○○ T-NAUGHTY 📶　　7:27 PM　　✻ 23% 🔋

BIG FOREHEADS
NAUGHTY TINDER CHATS

> Hey babe? What you up to tonight?

> Hey :) just doing uni work. What about you?

> Look... I'm gonna be honest with you.. I'm really keen on fatties with big foreheads. When are we doing this?

Send

OUT OF PRISON
NAUGHTY TINDER CHATS

> Hi just got out of prison and my parents changed the locks so I could really use a place to stay

> you're cute by the way

> What the fuck?

DISOBEDIENT AVOCADO
NAUGHTY TINDER CHATS

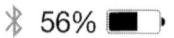

> Hey there

> Hey. I want to smear you in green paint and spank you like a disobedient avocado.

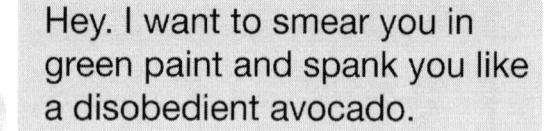

NO CHAIRS?
NAUGHTY TINDER CHATS

Hey how are you?

I'm great! You?

I'm exhausted personally, just had to get rid of every single chair in my house.

.....Why?

So that when you come over you have no choice but to sit on my face.

What's your number babe?

It would be hard to tell you to take a seat and chill since you took all of the chairs out of your

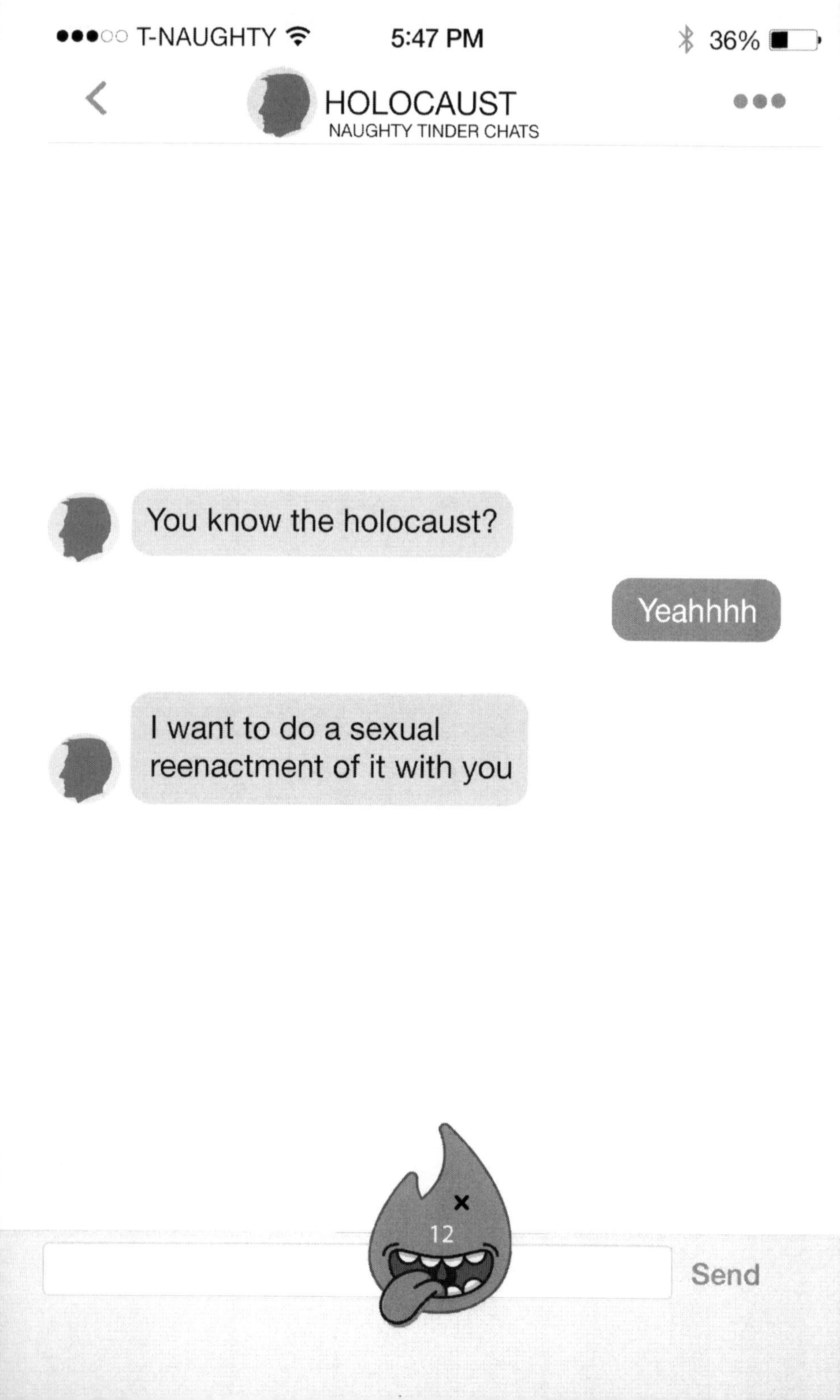
T-NAUGHTY
5:47 PM
36%
HOLOCAUST
NAUGHTY TINDER CHATS
You know the holocaust?
Yeahhhh
I want to do a sexual reenactment of it with you
12
Send

•••○○ T-NAUGHTY 📶   6:40 PM   ✳ 33% 🔋

JUDGING
NAUGHTY TINDER CHATS

> Judging by your gasses, you seem like a girl who likes anal. What's your number

Send

●●●○○ T-NAUGHTY 📶   5:56 PM   ✱ 94% 🔋

DRAGONS
NAUGHTY TINDER CHATS

> Do you like dragons?

> Sure.... Why?

> Good. Cuz I'm gonna be dragon my balls across your face tonight.

Send

●●●○○ T-NAUGHTY 📶 5:49 PM 35% 🔋

TAPES & CDs
NAUGHTY TINDER CHATS

Do you like tapes and cds?

Yeahhhh

Good, I'm going to tape my dick to your forhead so that you can cds nuts

Send

●●●○○ T-NAUGHTY 📶 3:29 PM ※ 29% 🔋

< **MY WIFE**
NAUGHTY TINDER CHATS •••

Hey there :)

Hi there! How are you?

I'm good, just watching TV with my wife

Ignore that!!! :)

I don't have a wife..lol

Send

••●○○ T-NAUGHTY 🛜　　7:29 PM　　🔵 73% 🔋

100% OFF
NAUGHTY TINDER CHATS

I'm having a sale at my place this weekend, all clothes 100% off, you in?

Send

ALPHABET
NAUGHTY TINDER CHATS

> If you could rearrange the alphabet, do yu know what I'd do?

Lol what woul you do?

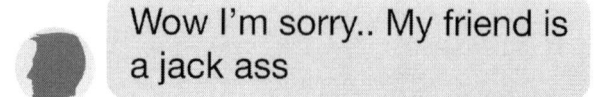

> I would put my p in your v

> Wow I'm sorry.. My friend is a jack ass

Maybe the alphabet should stay the way it is ... with n next to o.

> Haha I'm not going to try to recover from that but your response was damn good.

I'M JEWISH
NAUGHTY TINDER CHATS

If you right leg was Christmas and your left leg was Easter, would you let me come for dinner between the holidays?

I'm jewish!

●●●○○ T-NAUGHTY 📶　　5:41 PM　　✻ 36% 🔋

< 　　**PEARL HARBOR?**　　●●●
　　NAUGHTY TINDER CHATS

Down for playing Pearl Harbor ? I'll lie back and be the ship and you can blow me away. :)

Send

FROZEN YOGHURT
NAUGHTY TINDER CHATS

> I'll be in the neighborhood later I was wondering if you wanted to get some frozen yoghurt, or a whole meal, if that would be agreeable

> And by frozen yoghurt, I mean your vagina in my face.

> And there it is

> Haha I tried playing nice

●●●○○ T-NAUGHTY 2:59 PM 99%

DUCK
NAUGHTY TINDER CHATS

Wanna see my duck?

Yeap

Sorry i meant dick! :D

Nope

Send

●●●○○ T-NAUGHTY 📶   3:23 PM   ✱ 96% 🔋

FETTUCCINI
NAUGHTY TINDER CHATS

> Lets fuck :D

> Im eating fettuccini alfredo right now im kinda busy

> My dick better then fettuccini

Send

T-NAUGHTY
4:11 PM
95%
DIRTY LOAD
NAUGHTY TINDER CHATS
Are you a washing machine?
Yeah
Good because I wanna fill you with dirty load :P
Jesus Christ!
24
Send

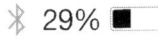

JELLY & JAM
NAUGHTY TINDER CHATS

> What's the difference between jam and jelly?

> Ohh clever. Well I know the difference. Jam has whole fruit pieces

> Nope. The real difference is that I can't jelly my dick in your ass

●●●○○ T-NAUGHTY 📶　　3:24 PM　　　※ 27% 🔋

< 　　**ARCHAELOGIST**
　　　NAUGHTY TINDER CHATS　　●●●

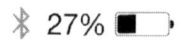

> Are you by chance an archaelogist?

> Because I have a really average sized bone i'd like you to inspect.

>> Been so long since it was in use that an archaelogist has to look at it?

●●●○○ T-NAUGHTY 📶   9:46 PM   ⁂ 97% 🔋

RENAISSANCE
NAUGHTY TINDER CHATS

Hey you.

Hello yourself. What were you and your friends dressed up for in one of your pics ?

Renaissance. If you were my homework I would slam you on my desk, do you for three hours, realize I've been doing it wrong, cry myself to sleep and wake up late to class the morning after

Send

●●●○○ T-NAUGHTY 📶   6:33 PM   ❊ 99% 🔋

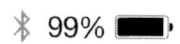

WANNA FU**
NAUGHTY TINDER CHATS

> Hey do you wanna fuck I am horny!

> You shoul've started with a hello

> Hello

> Do you wanna fuck I am horny!

Send

CRAZY WALK
NAUGHTY TINDER CHATS

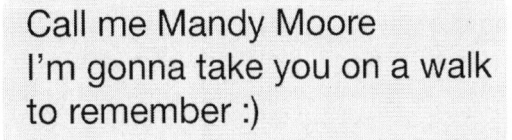

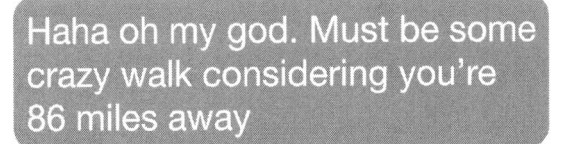

> Call me Mandy Moore I'm gonna take you on a walk to remember :)

> Haha oh my god. Must be some crazy walk considering you're 86 miles away

> fuck frankly I'd do anything at this point. I've got a yellow fever and the only way I can see it being cured is if I stick my egg roll into your bowl of rice. Please this isn't a joke.

WORSHIP
NAUGHTY TINDER CHATS

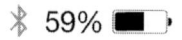

I want to worship your clit

Interesting approach

Now is it effective is the question?

Well has it worked before?

Yeah, but I'm going for a higher success rate :)

BOILING WATER
NAUGHTY TINDER CHATS

I would dip my balls in boiling water just to smell the desk you sat in in 5th grade.

●●●○○ T-NAUGHTY 📶　　6:25 PM　　🔵 41% 🔋

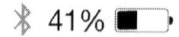

FAT BIT**
NAUGHTY TINDER CHATS

I wanna lick Nutella off you booty

No thank you

Fine lick it off mine fat bitch

Send

ELEVATOR
NAUGHTY TINDER CHATS

If you were an elevator, what button would I have to press to get you to go down?

> It's always a good chat up line when it starts with "if you were an elevator"

I think it'd be an honour to be an elevator.

you'd always have people inside you....

●●●○○ T-NAUGHTY 📶   6:39 PM   🔵 72% 🔋

JEWISH CUM
NAUGHTY TINDER CHATS

How'd you like some Jewish cum on your face?

Send

●●●○○ T-NAUGHTY 📶 5:14 PM 19% 🔋

PULLED OVER
NAUGHTY TINDER CHATS

> I just got pulled over by a cop writing my initial response. He gave me the whole "texting and driving is dangerous bla bla blah" speech and was about to give me a ticket. But I showed him your picture and explained what Tinder was. He let me off with a warning and said I better get your number.

Send

●●●○○ T-NAUGHTY 📶   9:16 PM   ✳ 97% 🔋

BEYONCE & OPRAH
NAUGHTY TINDER CHATS

> Would you rather piss off Beyonce or Oprah? Based solely on their potential to make you disappear

> Mmmm good question. Oprah. I cloud not love with myself if I pissed off queen beyonce.

> Live

> I bet you could love with yourself if you closed your eyes and thought about Ryan Gosling

Send

•••○○ T-NAUGHTY 📶 3:44 PM ✱ 57% 🔋

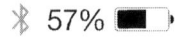

BIRD OF PEACE
NAUGHTY TINDER CHATS

the dove is the bird of peace do you know the bird of love??

Manatee

The swallow

Send

FAMILY REUNION
NAUGHTY TINDER CHATS

> Are we far removed 2nd cousins?

> Hahahaha I don't think so why?

> Aw man I only hookup with girls at my family reunion. Pure blood and all that....

> Hahaha well guess I don't make the cut then

> That's too bad cause you look like my sister and that is HOT

ARROGANCE
NAUGHTY TINDER CHATS

> Nicole, you're beatiful. Have you ever dated a guy more attractive than yourself, and if not, can I be your first?Have

> Ewwww, I totally just saw this message. Arrogance, huh? lol

●●●○○ T-NAUGHTY 📶   5:19 PM   ❋ 21% 🔋

BIG THICK DI*
NAUGHTY TINDER CHATS

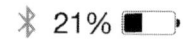

I got a big thick dick and was wondering if you wanted to see it of something?

Send

T-NAUGHTY 6:09 PM 40%

JADE MONKEY
NAUGHTY TINDER CHATS

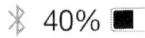

> You must find the jade monkey before the next full moon.

> It is imperative to the quest.

> Actually sir, We found the jade monkey it was in your glove compartment.

> Marry me.

> Haha, could I delay the response to a time of convenience for both our parties?

> Don't try and change me baby.

41

Send

NUDES?
NAUGHTY TINDER CHATS

Hey I got to tell you something.

Okay

Nudes?

Wow you really know how to make a girl feel special don't you?

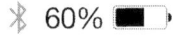

ADVICE ON BL**JOB
NAUGHTY TINDER CHATS

What will you give me for $60

Relationship advice

How about a blowjob

I guess I could give you advice on blowjobs

No you physically give me a blowjob

Advice on physically receiving a blowjob?

CRAB
NAUGHTY TINDER CHATS

> DAMN girl are you crab cause I wanna crack open those legs

FALL FROM HEAVEN
NAUGHTY TINDER CHATS

Did you fall from heaven...? Becaue, have sex with me?

Sorry didn't suffer a head injury during the fall

SHRIMP
NAUGHTY TINDER CHATS

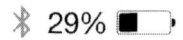

> How are you?

Good U?

> I'd like to put my shrimp on your barbie, if you know what I mean.

> I mean sex

> Hello????

MATH TEST
NAUGHTY TINDER CHATS

> What's 22+37?

I'm not a calculator mate, if you need help with simple sums I suggest you go to a maths tutor.

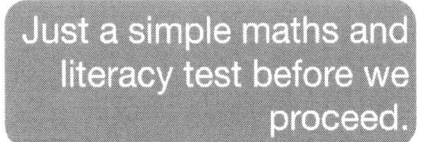

> Just a simple maths and literacy test before we proceed.

> In what situation would you use whom over who?

FALL FROM HEAVEN
NAUGHTY TINDER CHATS

> I bet your orgasm face is amazing :) just saying

ILLITERATE
NAUGHTY TINDER CHATS

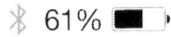

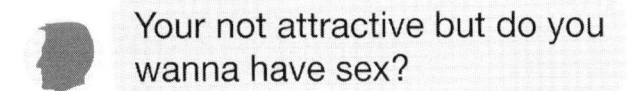

Your not attractive but do you wanna have sex?

HAHAHAHA *you're

buut rilly Lillian

are you illiterate

lehmme set babey kaces

Ok yes you are

IMPOLITE ASSHO**
NAUGHTY TINDER CHATS

Ayyy girl

Would you like to try that again??

Would you like to try this dick?

No!

Damn you are rude as fuck

I'm rude because I refuse to fuck an impolite asshole? You should reevaluate.

Hahah I just was being rude to break the ice but now that were comfortable. How are u doing?

●●●○○ T-NAUGHTY 📶　　3:13 PM　　　 ✳ 88% 🔋

MASTERBAT**G
NAUGHTY TINDER CHATS

What up?

> Just catching up some Game of Thrones! You?

Great show

I'm masterbating

Send

DONATE A PICTURE
NAUGHTY TINDER CHATS

I dont mean o offend you. But would you donate a picture of your tits for charity?

Is this a hypothetical situation or a request

Yes

Not a yes or no question

Okay

••●○○ T-NAUGHTY 🛜   3:29 PM   ✶ 28% ▪

PLACE TO SIT
NAUGHTY TINDER CHATS

Hey baby, as long as I have a face, you'll have a place to sit

Send

●●●○○ T-NAUGHTY 📶　　4:28 PM　　※ 53% 🔋

RIDE YOU LIKE...
NAUGHTY TINDER CHATS

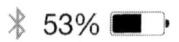

> Hey there :) nothing much, you?

Do you still have braids ?

> Yeah haha, I got them done not too long ago

May I grab onto them like reins and ride you like a horse ?

Send

••●○○ T-NAUGHTY 5:29 PM 24%

BMW & 9INCH
NAUGHTY TINDER CHATS

Hello

how are you doing ?

do you want to hook up, I have BMW 2014 and 9inches dick and some 420 :)

Hello

Send

•••○○ T-NAUGHTY 📶   8:18 PM   ✴ 67% 🔋

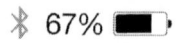

WATERMELON
NAUGHTY TINDER CHATS

> If I were a watermelon would you spit or swallow my seeds? :D

Send

●●●○○ T-NAUGHTY 4:28 PM 52% 🔋

SCHOOL TOMORROW
NAUGHTY TINDER CHATS

> Whats the difference between you and school tomorrow?

What

> I'm not gonna come into school tomorrow

Send

●●●○○ T-NAUGHTY 📶   7:49 PM   ✱ 94% 🔋

PURITY RING
NAUGHTY TINDER CHATS

> Hey

Heyy

> What are you doing?

Not too much just relaxiing you?

> Same here. What are you wearing?

My purity ring

Send

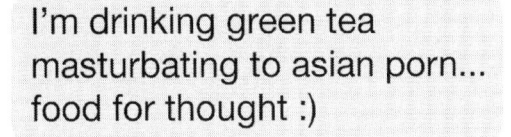

FOOD FOR THOUGHT
NAUGHTY TINDER CHATS

Hi

I'm drinking green tea masturbating to asian porn... food for thought :)

SARCASM?
NAUGHTY TINDER CHATS

> Hey how about you be my story and ill be your climax ?

Wow haven't heard that one before

> Sarcasm? Aha

No I've literally never heard that before

•••○○ T-NAUGHTY 🛜 3:19 PM ✳ 86% 🔋

OVERSIZED CLIT***
NAUGHTY TINDER CHATS

> What are your views on scissoring?? Because I can tuck into a pretty fantastic loocking mangina and we could go at it for 30 mins... Orange is the new black style

As a bi sexual female I've never really got the scissoring thing but with you who knows you may blow my socks off

> Just think of my penis as an oversized clitoros

Send

•••○○ T-NAUGHTY 📶   5:29 PM   ⁕ 28% 🔋

CHICKEN FINGERS
NAUGHTY TINDER CHATS

> What are you here looking around for?

> honestly????

> Blowjobs chicken fingers and anal. Not in that order.

Send

●●●○○ T-NAUGHTY 📶   3:14 PM   ❊ 29% ◼

ANIMAL SEXLIFE
NAUGHTY TINDER CHATS

If you sexlife was an animal what would it be?

Dead

Send

WINTER
NAUGHTY TINDER CHATS

Is your name winter? Because you'll be coming soon :)

I hope your sake that this pickup line is not representative of your abilities in bed because winter is still 6 month away and that's a really long time to come

•••○○ T-NAUGHTY 📶　　1:21 AM　　🔵 64% 🔋

WALKIE TALKIE
NAUGHTY TINDER CHATS

> I would drag my balls across 2 miles of broken glass just to hear you queef through a walkie-talkie

Send

●●●○○ T-NAUGHTY 📶　　2:59 PM　　※ 47% 🔋

SEMI HOT
NAUGHTY TINDER CHATS

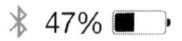

Im a hot indian, you a semi hot indian. Lets meet up and create beautiful babyies

I don't think calling girls semi hot is gonna get you laid :/

Ehh its better than calling you hot, that would just inflate your ego. When are you free?

•••○○ T-NAUGHTY 📶　　1:14 PM　　※ 85% 🔋

DUCK SIZED HORSE
NAUGHTY TINDER CHATS

> Would you rather fight 100 duck sized horses or 1 horse sized dick?

> 100 duck sized horses, that giant duck beak could do some damage

> so true

> are you horny?

Send

80 MILES
NAUGHTY TINDER CHATS

> BLOWJOB?

> Why the fuck would I drive 80 miles to put your dick in my mouth ????!!??

> Haha that's awesome that you assumed you'd have to do the driving

ASIAN GIRL
NAUGHTY TINDER CHATS

> You are by far the sexiest asian girl ive ever seen

> Jokes on you cuz I'm not asian

> Still sexy

SWITCH BRAINS
NAUGHTY TINDER CHATS

Hey :)

That was an inappropriate amount of smileys

Sorry I never know how many to do :(

ohhh... awkward

:(

Do you think that if two people made out hard enough they could switch brains?

ANGEL OR ANGLE
NAUGHTY TINDER CHATS

You look like an angle

Lol an angle or an angel ?

No I mean angle. You have a very sculpted jaw structure

•••○○ T-NAUGHTY 📶　　6:15 PM　　※ 69% 🔋

FIRST DATE
NAUGHTY TINDER CHATS

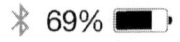

So how are you ging to impress me on ur first date?

I'll show up

•••○○ T-NAUGHTY 📶　　2:41 AM　　* 62% 🔋

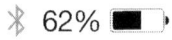

BIG CO**
NAUGHTY TINDER CHATS

> Do you like men with big cocks?

> Yes

> Sorry I wasted your time.

Send

COFFEE LOVER
NAUGHTY TINDER CHATS

> What does coffee and pussy have in common?

> Uhhm idk what ? Haha!

> They both know how to get me "up" in the morning. Not my best but it was original.

> And ur a coffee lover so used that.

IDK = "I Don't Know"

HOGWARTS EXPRESS
NAUGHTY TINDER CHATS

> Did you know they call my nob the hogwarts express ?

> And why is that then?

> Because its 9 nd 3 quaters :)

> cm obviously, not inches

LAID ON TINDER
NAUGHTY TINDER CHATS

How do i get laid on tinder?

Oh shit this isn't google

Hahaha that I like

Well google didn't help so do you think you can?

I'm pretty sure it'll be easy for you

BIG NOSE?
NAUGHTY TINDER CHATS

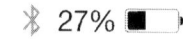

I'd break all the chairs in the world so you'd have to sit on my face

Why? Is your nose bigger than your dick?

•••○○ T-NAUGHTY 📶　　　6:02 PM　　　* 81% 🔋

< 　　　**PORN STAR**　　　•••
　　　NAUGHTY TINDER CHATS

Is your friend in the first picture a porn star, she look really familiar? I think I worked with her a few years ago.

Seeing as that's my 16 year old sister, I dont think you worked with her a few years ago.

Send

IN THE EAR
NAUGHTY TINDER CHATS

Hey how's it going?

In the ear!

What's your favorite way to get fuxed?

Send

PUMA PANTS
NAUGHTY TINDER CHATS

> Knock knock

Whose there?

> Puma

Puma who?

> You gotta give me your number or Imma going to puma pants

MISSING BLOW***
NAUGHTY TINDER CHATS

I seem to have left a blowjob in your house. When i can come and collect it?

I had a look for it, but couldn't see it anywhere

SPELL HUMOR
NAUGHTY TINDER CHATS

I wanna sniff coke off your pussy

What a romatic first date

<3

Like a girl who can handle humore

I like a guy who can spell humor

WRONG WAY
NAUGHTY TINDER CHATS

> Congratulations. You have a great taste in men!

> I'm new to tinder, I swiped the wrong way.

MECHANICAL BULL
NAUGHTY TINDER CHATS

Would you ride my face like a mechanical bull?

Does that line ever work?

Nope lol

Didn't think so

:(

ROSES OR DAISIES?
NAUGHTY TINDER CHATS

> Roses or Daisies?

> Daisies

> Ok I was just wondering what to put on your casket after I murder that pussy

●●●○○ T-NAUGHTY 📶 2:56 PM ✴ 94% 🔋

UGLIEST KIDS?
NAUGHTY TINDER CHATS

> Which sex position produces the ugliest kids?

> Ughh I don't know? loool

> Ask your parents

> WTF???????!

WTF = "what the fuck"

Send

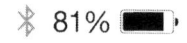

POOP OUT TOAST
NAUGHTY TINDER CHATS

Hey hey hey hey..

You're so hot that if you ate bread you'd poop out toast

●●●○○ T-NAUGHTY 📶 7:56 PM ✱ 30% 🔋

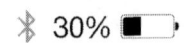

BUILD A BEAR
NAUGHTY TINDER CHATS

Do you work at build a bear ?

No why?

Cause I'd stuff you haha

Haha. You're really cute tho

Haha how clever

Send

BALLOON NOISE
NAUGHTY TINDER CHATS

> All of my family came to visit and we hadn't all been together in like.... years lol

Ohh that's awesome!

> Yeah it was nice! So tell me something exciting about yourself :)

Is it bad that I wish I was on my knees in front of you right now

> Whaat?

Just figured I could do anything that you wanted wanted :)

> *deflating balloon noise*

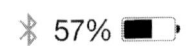

PICK YOU UP
NAUGHTY TINDER CHATS

> Wanna go for coffee?

Wooo alright..

Sure!

> Ok my dad get's home at 6 so we'll drive over then and pick you up.

> ?? I need your address

●●●○○ T-NAUGHTY 📶 7:24 PM ⁕ 48% 🔋

ACRONYM
NAUGHTY TINDER CHATS

I made a new acronym.

RTB :)

Whattt?

READY TO BANG

Ohhhh

Yep! So flattering right

that's a good one Oo

Send

GARBAGE
NAUGHTY TINDER CHATS

Are you garbage? Cause I wanna take you out

●●●○○ T-NAUGHTY 📶   6:12 PM   ✳ 83% 🔋

PLANETS
NAUGHTY TINDER CHATS

> Hey guuuuurrrl!!! There's only three planets tonight. Because I'm destroying your anus.

Send

SLINKY
NAUGHTY TINDER CHATS

Are you a turkey?

No, why?

Well you just look like you could use a good stuffing

Are you a slinky?

Cause you need a good push down the stairs

DOUCHE
NAUGHTY TINDER CHATS

> Hey, so they call me big D. The D doesn't stand for Daniel :)

> Does it stand for douche?

A GOOD VIBE
NAUGHTY TINDER CHATS

> You look sort of like a slut but in a good way

> A good vibe

> Oh wow that's my cue to stop talking to you

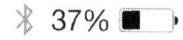

BATH WATER
NAUGHTY TINDER CHATS

> Holy fuck, I'd love to drink your bath warer

> Holy fuck, I'd love for u to drink my bath water

> That's disgusting!

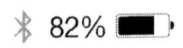

BABY DIC*
NAUGHTY TINDER CHATS

Hey !

Wanna see my dick?

NOPE!

What if it's really small and will make u laugh?

Wanna see my baby dick?

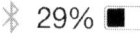

MANNEQUIN
NAUGHTY TINDER CHATS

> Does your carpet match your drapery?

Loooool gross

> But actually though. I need to know for the mannequin doll of you I'm making

I'm never leaving my house again

> Good to know :)

•••○○ T-NAUGHTY 🛜   2:42 AM   ❋ 63% 🔋

PINKY TOE
NAUGHTY TINDER CHATS

> You remind me of my pinky toe: small, cute and I'm probably going to bang you on the coffee table tonight.

Send

ANAL
NAUGHTY TINDER CHATS

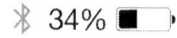

Anal?

When it comes to organizing my closet, yes.

T-NAUGHTY 7:11 PM 43%

STUFF BEAVER
NAUGHTY TINDER CHATS

Do you know anything about taxidermy? Because I can show you how to stuff a beaver.

Haha.... Nice :)

102

Send

SOPHIA ?!
NAUGHTY TINDER CHATS

> Hey Sophia, I'm Phil, nice to digitally meet you! You are very pretty aesthetically.

My name is Sarah...

BANG & HANG
NAUGHTY TINDER CHATS

Just visiting lol. I'm only here for a soccer game then I leave Wednesday morning!

Nice, have fun!

Thanks we should bang before I leave!

Hang*

Haha nice typo :D

Hahah you caught on! And i got a hotel room

BEST OPENING LINE
NAUGHTY TINDER CHATS

> Ready for my best opening line ?

> Here it comes....

> _____

> Haha you made me laugh I'll give you that.

> Best opening line I've seen

> If that made you laugh wait until you see my penis

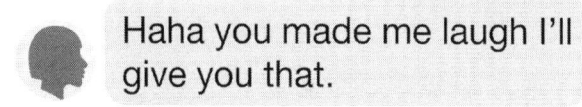

FART CHIMNEY
NAUGHTY TINDER CHATS

> Nice dumper girl

Right?!

> I'd dive head first into that!!
>
> I wanna sweep your fart chimney

lol laaaaawdie lawd. Please stop!

> So it that a no?

●●●○○ T-NAUGHTY 📶   8:13PM   ✳ 87% 🔋

FAV. POSITION
NAUGHTY TINDER CHATS

> Hey do you have a favorite sex position hahah?

> No?

Kneeling on my knees praying to our lord and savior

Send

BUTT STUFF
NAUGHTY TINDER CHATS

> 20 Question? U first !

Favourite type of cuisine?

Easy one to start

> Greek! Ever done butt stuff?

Haha I haven't!

Number one fantasy?

> butt stuff

KILL HITLER!
NAUGHTY TINDER CHATS

> Fuck one, marry one, Kill one. Me, Hitler and me again. Go!

Hahah good one. Fuck you, marry you and kill Hitler!

> Well now that I know you're not a Nazi, I suppose we can get down to business here.

Hahah you're so right.

●●●○○ T-NAUGHTY 📶   4:14 PM   ✷ 45% 🔋

REAL LOVE?
NAUGHTY TINDER CHATS

> Do you think love is a real thing?

> > I think that's the beginning of an interesting conversation. You first.

> I don't think anything is real. Everything is a construct of my diseased mind.

> I am alone inside my head

> Wanna get coffee ?

Send

•••○○ T-NAUGHTY 📶　　3:42 AM　　　＊ 65% 🔋

SNOW MAN
NAUGHTY TINDER CHATS

What do a snow man say to another?

I don't know

I can smell carrot

Send

●●●○○ T-NAUGHTY 📶　　8:37 PM　　🔵 17% 🔋

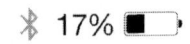

CUDDLING
NAUGHTY TINDER CHATS

> Are you a good cuddler? I might let you join my gang

>> Really? Ya def put me down I might make the cut

> Gimme your number and we'll start cuddling ppl HARD

PPL = people
DEF = definitely

Send

BREAKFAST
NAUGHTY TINDER CHATS

> If you were a sandwich what would be on you

Bacon and egg. Because the best food is breakfast food and that's a breakfast sandwich. Do you always start conversations so oddly?

> You have no idea.

EGYPTIAN SKATER
NAUGHTY TINDER CHATS

> Haha impressive..

> What did you really major in?

Hypothetical Egyptian Skater Culture

My thesis was about whether King Tut could do a sick kick flip

I'm $300.000 in debt

> Whaaatt?!

HEADLESS
NAUGHTY TINDER CHATS

> How do yu feel about antique dolls?

I prefer them headless

> But then they can't watch

•••○○ T-NAUGHTY 📶   8:13PM   ✳ 87% 🔋

WIENER
NAUGHTY TINDER CHATS

> How small was the tiniest wiener you have ever seen?

> Get ready to be topped.

Send

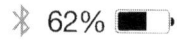

GROCERIES
NAUGHTY TINDER CHATS

I like my girls I like my groceries

From an organic market? lol

Nah. In a bag in my trunk

WHAT'S UR NAME
NAUGHTY TINDER CHATS

Hey :)

Hey what's your name?

Alice :)

Oh that's a nice name, how do you spell that?

You're hilarious! Really!

Oh that's not even nearly how I usually spell it.

STRANGE CLOWN
NAUGHTY TINDER CHATS

> Have you ever seen that clown at Walmart that hides from gay people?

No?

> HAHAHAHAHAHAHA!!!!!!!

......shit!

●●●○○ T-NAUGHTY 📶   9:33 PM   ✱ 17% 🔋

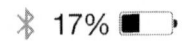

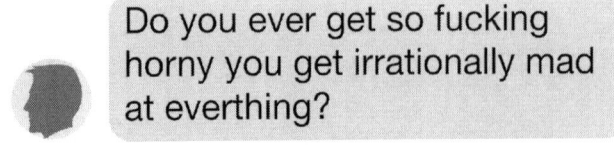

WEIRD GUY
NAUGHTY TINDER CHATS

> Do you ever get so fucking horny you get irrationally mad at everthing?

> Sorry this is a really weird question but I want to see if I'm not the only fucking one.

> I'd recommend some alone time

120

Send

GERMANY 1942
NAUGHTY TINDER CHATS

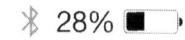

> On a scale of 1 to America, how free are you tonight?

Germany, 1942!

BITC*
NAUGHTY TINDER CHATS

> Probably quite nice? I bet you're actually a stone cold bitch

> Wow. I really don't enjoy being called a bitch, so I am not even sure how to respond to that man.

> You slap me/throw your drink in my face? Business as usual?

●●●○○ T-NAUGHTY 📶   1:40 PM   ≭ 64% 🔋

LOOKING CUTE
NAUGHTY TINDER CHATS

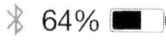

> Hey how was your weekend?

> I would totally let you take me to brunch tomorrow

> This is so us. Me doing all the talking and you sitting there looking cute

Loooool

Send

DENTAL FLOSS
NAUGHTY TINDER CHATS

I would padle a cross the Atlantic ocean in a canoe made of hardened elephant foreskin with only the Mexican soccer teams post game sweat as my water supply if it meant I could lace my shoes with your used dental floss

●●●○○ T-NAUGHTY 📶 8:27 PM 24% 🔋

WONDERSTRUCK
NAUGHTY TINDER CHATS

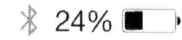

> Hey how's your day going so far?

> I'm wonderstruck, blushing all the way home

> Lol why is that ?

Send

DRINK
NAUGHTY TINDER CHATS

> Sorry, but you owe me a drink.

> Why?

> Because when I looked at you, I dropped mine.

MEAT MARKET
NAUGHTY TINDER CHATS

> If this app is a meat market, you must be the prime rib.

●●●○○ T-NAUGHTY 📶   9:14 PM   ✴ 41% 🔋

TERRORISTS
NAUGHTY TINDER CHATS

Hey are you a middle eastern dictator?

I don't negotiate with terrorists

Because there's a political uprising in my pants.

Send

COCAINE
NAUGHTY TINDER CHATS

> Hey, tell me something about yourself that other guys wouldn't know

> I'm a huge fan of cocaine

•••○○ T-NAUGHTY 8:52 PM 18%

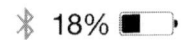

THROAT
NAUGHTY TINDER CHATS

> Like cock down your throat?

> WTF is wrong with you?

> You look like someone that does

WTF = What the fuck

Send

SLAM?
NAUGHTY TINDER CHATS

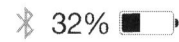

You are a slam

A what?

Slam piece: anyone you would never marry or date, but would fuck into the Andromeda galaxy.

•••○○ T-NAUGHTY 📶 1:53 AM ✱ 61% 🔋

< **KITTY**
NAUGHTY TINDER CHATS

> Ohh I'm allergic to cats, I was referring to the other kitty lol

Sorry I only have on kitty

> Are you a ranny that loves cats?

Send

HAUNTED HOUSE
NAUGHTY TINDER CHATS

> If you were a haunted house, I'd cry if I came inside of you

Everybody cries when the come inside me

Just ask your dad

> If you're anything like your mother then I already know why

Touche

●●●○○ T-NAUGHTY 📶　　9:14PM　　　✳ 82% 🔋

< 　　　**EAT ASS ?**　　　●●●
　　　　NAUGHTY TINDER CHATS

Do you eat ass?

Not my thing

Ohh. well I do

What's your number?

315-XXXXXXX

Send

WEIRD QUESTION
NAUGHTY TINDER CHATS

> How would you like to be disposed of when you're dead?

Weird question!!!

> Like to be buried in a large satin-lined coffin, with a couple of Page Three stunners. They're alive..

U don't have other things to talk about?

> Ok. Two questions. How are we going to eat, and what floor's the restaurant on?

MILLIONS
NAUGHTY TINDER CHATS

> If I received a penny for everytime I saw someone as beautiful as you, I'd have millions of $

KANGAROO
NAUGHTY TINDER CHATS

Are you Australian? Because you meet all of my kangaroo-fications.

FULL COLOR EDITION

GORDON SUTHERLAND

DAMN YOU FAT FINGERS

BEST TYPING MISTAKES AND AUTOCORRECT FAILS

Vulgar, perverted, politically incorrect and absolutely Lol

WHAT SHOULD I READ NEXT?

ISBN 10: 1499599498   ISBN 13: 978-1499599497

T-Correct
06:06
93%
DAMN YOU FAT FINGERS
Vulgar, perverted, politically incorrect and absolutely Lol
I just swallowed a huge piece of bubble gum. Is that a big deal?
You´ll be fine. I have swallowed so much cum in my life and I´m still here.
I didn´t need to know that mom!
Dear lord, that was a word changed by my phone!
Sure, mom was a slut. haha
FAT FINGERS ARE TYPING
Send

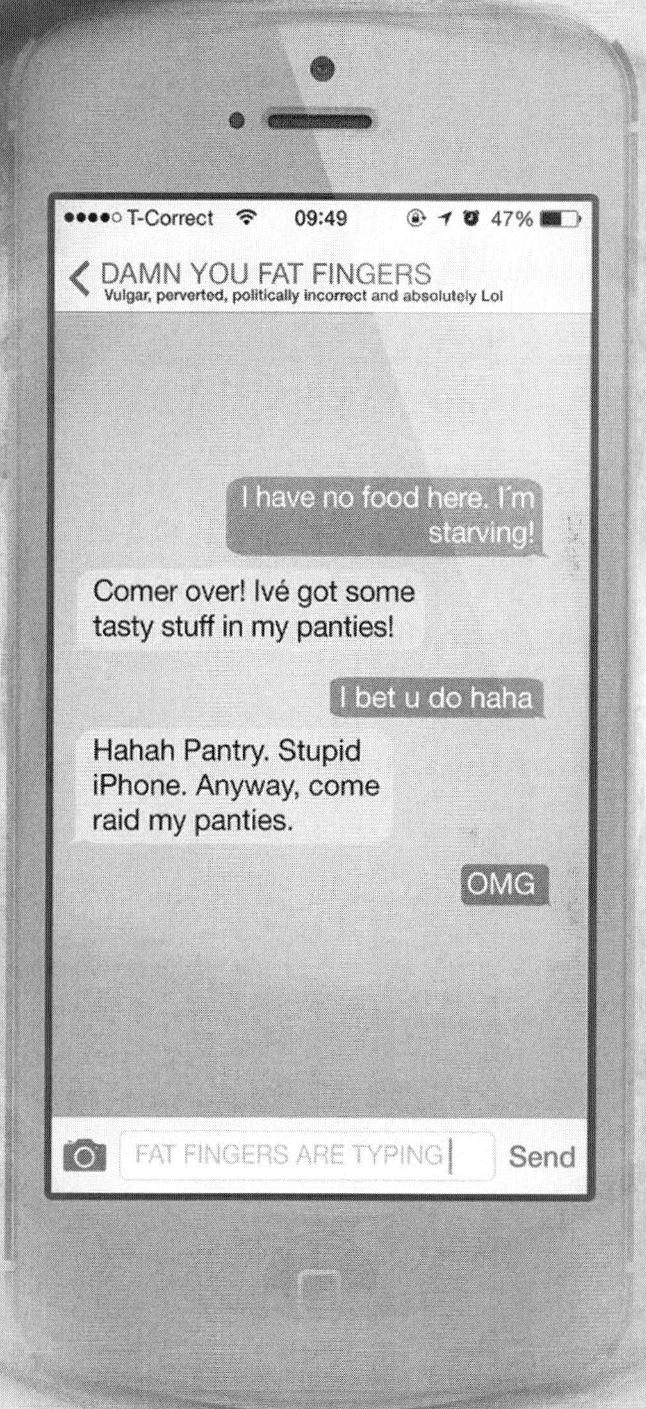

●●●●○ T-Correct
09:49
47%
DAMN YOU FAT FINGERS
Vulgar, perverted, politically incorrect and absolutely Lol
I have no food here. I´m starving!
Comer over! Ivé got some tasty stuff in my panties!
I bet u do haha
Hahah Pantry. Stupid iPhone. Anyway, come raid my panties.
OMG
FAT FINGERS ARE TYPING
Send

●●●●○ T-Correct 10:19 98%
DAMN YOU FAT FINGERS
Vulgar, perverted, politically incorrect and absolutely Lol
So how was the date last night?
Did you score?
Not quite. First date we went to dinner and then walked her home.
then i killed her in the woods outside her house and left.
Killing here seems a bit harsh. Did she order the lobster and filet mignon at dinner or something ?
Kissed!!! WTF
FAT FINGERS ARE TYPING
Send

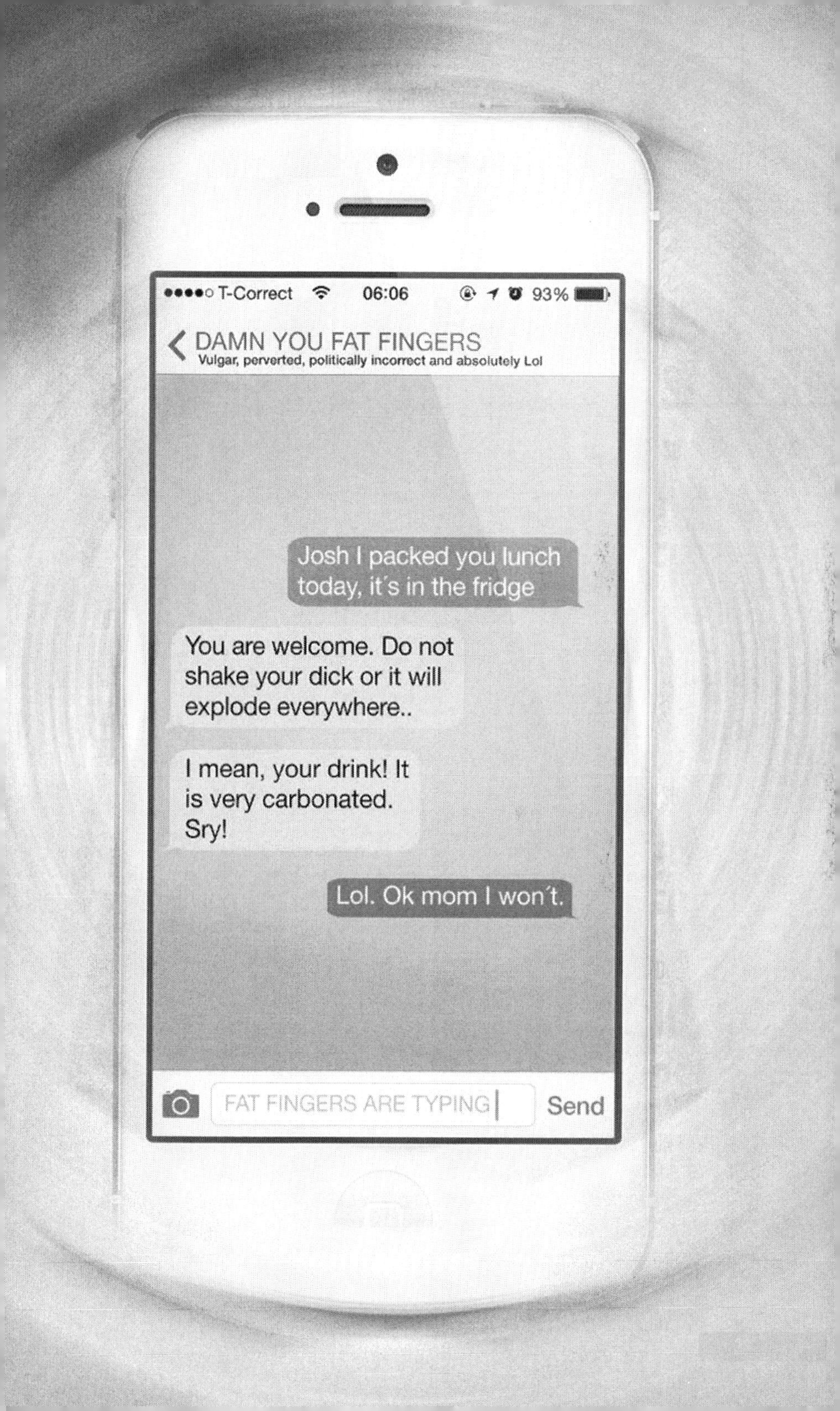
T-Correct
06:06
93%
DAMN YOU FAT FINGERS
Vulgar, perverted, politically incorrect and absolutely Lol
Josh I packed you lunch today, it´s in the fridge
You are welcome. Do not shake your dick or it will explode everywhere..
I mean, your drink! It is very carbonated. Sry!
Lol. Ok mom I won´t.
FAT FINGERS ARE TYPING
Send

Printed in Great Britain
by Amazon